HOLY WAR!
UNDERSTANDING RELIGIONS IN PUTIN'S RUSSIA

PANEL HELD AT THE MEETING OF THE DIVISION OF HUMANITIES AND SOCIAL SCIENCES OF THE AUSTRIAN ACADEMY OF SCIENCES ON 11 APRIL 2024

ÖAW

CONTENT

EDITORIAL

CHRISTIANE WENDEHORST | President of the Division of Humanities and Social Sciences, OeAW 5

CONTRIBUTIONS

PAOLO SARTORI | Senior Research Associate, Institute of Iranian Studies, OeAW
The Use and Abuse of Institutions: On Muslim Patriotism in Russia 7

GULNAZ SIBGATULLINA | Assistant Professor, Department of History, European Studies and Religion Studies, University of Amsterdam
Islam in Russia's Domestic and Foreign Policy after 2022 15

KRISTINA STOECKL | Professor of Sociology, Libera Università Internazionale degli Studi Sociali (Luiss), Rome
Religion, Law and Politics for a Russia at War 27

EDITORIAL

CHRISTIANE WENDEHORST

The Austrian Academy of Sciences is committed to serving as a forum for interdisciplinary discussions. Thus, each division regularly extends invitations to members and guest speakers from other institutions to give lectures or contribute to panel discussions on a broad range of subjects. The present publication is largely based on the panel discussion "Holy War! Understanding Religions in Putin's Russia" held at the meeting of the Division of Humanities and Social Sciences on 11 April 2024. The event was conceptualised by our corresponding member Paolo Sartori, to whom I would like to extend my gratitude on this occasion. As an alumnus of the Young Academy and a corresponding member since 2023, he has been a stalwart addition to our division, currently serving as chairman of the commission *Study of Islam in Central Eurasia* (SICE) at the Austrian Academy of Sciences. The commission explores the social, intellectual, and political history of the Muslim communities inhabiting the Volga-Ural region, the North Caucasus, Siberia, the Kazakh Steppe, Central Asia, and Crimea from the fall of the Khanate of Kazan (1552) to the present day. It aims to establish itself as one of the major research initiatives in Europe and North America devoted to fundamental research on Islam in Central Eurasia, while at the same time seeking to integrate the study of the Muslims who inhabit these regions into the global history of Islam.[1]

The other panellists who contributed to this volume are Gulnaz Sibgatullina and Kristina Stoeckl. Gulnaz Sibgatullina is an assistant professor studying illiberal regimes in the Department of History, European

1 For more information, please see: https://www.oeaw.ac.at/sice/

Christiane Wendehorst is Professor of Private Law at the University of Vienna and Scientific Director of the European Law Institute (ELI). She has been President of the Humanities and Social Sciences Division of the Austrian Academy of Sciences since July 2022.

Studies and Religion Studies at the University of Amsterdam. Kristina Stoeckl is a professor of sociology at Luiss in Rome and an expert on religion-state relations in Russia. Like Paolo Sartori, she is a former member of the Young Academy. The three papers in this volume of *Akademie im Dialog – Forschung und Gesellschaft* impressively demonstrate the alliance of religion, nationalistic politics, ideology, and legislation that Russia has forged to 'legitimise' its war in the Ukraine. Interestingly, it is not only the Russian Orthodox Church that plays a role here, but also Islam, as Paolo Sartori's and Gulnaz Sibgatullina's papers discuss. Sartori, in his paper "The Use and Abuse of Institutions: On Muslim Patriotism in Russia" shows how confessional minorities, such as Muslims, were incorporated into the Russian identity over the centuries. Sibgatullina's paper "Islam in Russia's Domestic and Foreign Policy after 2022" explains how Islamic institutions contribute both domestically and internationally to the legitimacy of the current Russian regime. Kristina Stoeckl, in her contribution "Religion, Law and Politics for a Russia at War", focuses on how the Russian Orthodox Church became an ally of the autocratic state.

This volume provides ample and thought-provoking input on the role of religions in contemporary Russia—as did the panel discussion in April 2024. I am delighted that the thoughts and findings of the discussion are finally available in print, and I wish you an engaging and illuminating reading experience.

For the purpose of the present publication, the contributions have been edited and slightly abridged.

THE USE AND ABUSE OF INSTITUTIONS: ON MUSLIM PATRIOTISM IN RUSSIA

Paolo Sartori is a senior research associate at the Institute of Iranian Studies and a corresponding member of the Austrian Academy of Sciences. He specialises in the history of Central Asia and the Caucasus, especially under Tsarist and Soviet rule. An awardee of the START programme (FWF), he currently serves as the chairman of the commission Study of Islam in Central Eurasia *of the Austrian Academy of Sciences. His latest book is* A Soviet Sultanate: Islam in Socialist Uzbekistan, 1943-1991.

PAOLO SARTORI

More than three years have passed since Russia resolved to wage war against Ukraine, and such an all-out assault has been repeatedly branded as an existential war against a cast of evil characters ranging from Nazis and drug addicts to paedophiles and members of the LGTBQ community, all residing in Kyiv and coalescing around the government of Volodymyr Zelensky. On 9 March 2022, barely two weeks after the beginning of the invasion, Kirill, the patriarch of Moscow and primate of the Russian Orthodox Church, hurried to deliver a vitriolic sermon whereby he blessed the “special military operation” in Ukraine as a means for Russia to protect Eastern Christian values in a fight against the "morally depraved West" (Dijskra 2022). Kirill did not stop there, however; in a symbolic communion of the Russian army with the Orthodox Church, on 13 March 2022, following a liturgy conducted at the Cathedral of Christ the Saviour, the patriarch of Moscow entrusted the icon of Mary to the commander of the Russian National Guard to inspire the soldiers who take the oath to defend their motherland against Western corruption (Whalen 2022).

Kirill, however, has not been alone among religious authorities to present the war against Ukraine as part of a broader metaphysical mission. In fact, prior to him, on 27 February 2022, Salakh Mezhiev, the Grand Mufti of Chechnya, issued an online appeal calling the invasion of Ukraine a holy war (*jihad*). In a remarkable exegetic stretch, Mezhiev presented the actions of Vladimir Putin as similar to those of the Christian king of Abyssinia, who in the early days of Islam offered protection to the companions of the Prophet Muhammad, who were victims of persecution and consequently resolved to migrate to the Horn of Africa (Muhammad and Soliev 2023). Many have noted the ironic twist of history in the words of the Grand Mufti, of course: after two military campaigns in the last twenty-five years which have razed Grozny to the ground, brought destruction and death to the North Caucasus, and led to a massive diaspora from the region to Europe, to call Putin a protector of the Chechen people is undoubtedly a sign of unshakable loyalty to and faith in the Kremlin. Putin's weaponisation of religions to strengthen the ideology of the *Russkii Mir* ('the Russian World') has long been explained as a variation on the theme of alt-right nationalism. However, relatively little has been done to understand what lurks behind the loud bellicose voices rising from the Moscow Patriarchate, the various muftiates, and the priests blessing tanks and cluster bombs. Occasional observers usually explain the involvement of religious figures in instrumental terms, i.e, a way to appeal to the people for purposes of military mobilisation. While religious motives may push some to join the war effort, at the same time Russian citizens have fled the country in the hundreds of thousands to avoid the draft, thereby leaving the government to deploy convicts as cannon fodder; and yet icons have been repeatedly "toured around the front line" (Holl-Allen 2023) while Ukrainian drones often immortalise Russian soldiers as they beg for mercy while brandishing the image of the Holy Mary and making the sign of the cross.

In this volume of *Akademie im Dialog – Forschung und Gesellschaft* I propose to go beneath the crust of propaganda and unpack the religious components informing the ideology of the *Russkii Mir*. How are we to explain the phenomenon whereby religious institutions support authoritarianism and state violence on such a broad scale? Is patriotism the main motivation for young men to sign up to die? And if not, how are believers (Orthodox Christians, Muslims, and Buddhists) to make sense of the lethal embrace between confessional authorities and Putin's regime? What brings solace to the tens of thousands of families grieving over their dead? The money offered in exchange for voluntary conscription? The flamboyant Soviet past as embodied by Stalin? Or the ethereal afterlife promised by military chaplains and muftis? My fellow contributors to this volume will offer a number of reflections which may help us answer these questions. Within the limited space afforded to me by this paper, meanwhile, I shall confine myself to reconsidering how over the centuries Russia made space for and incorporated confessional minorities, especially Muslims, into the state.

When one is asked to describe the state of religion in Russia today, one usually thinks of the alliance between the Orthodox Church and the Russian state, an alliance whose purpose is to restore confidence as well as comfort the soul of the Russian people. And such an alliance is not just the imaginary projection of state-controlled media. Indeed, in 2016 Patriarch Kirill himself went so far as to claim that the Putin era is "a miracle of God"—a visionary insight that just so happened to occur to him after Putin agreed to take over expenses for the restoration of the patriarch's house in Moscow (Moscow Times 2019).

But religion in Russia can also have a different, less reassuring face: that of Shamil Basayev, an Islamist and terrorist who, between the 1990s and the early 2000s, undermined Russia's stability. Putin and Basayev wrestled for more than a decade in a brutal military confrontation that left Chechnya in dust, but which also put the solidity of Russia's statehood to the test. Basayev is of course notorious for a string of bombings at housing complexes, sieges of schools, theatres, and hospitals, and guerrilla fighters hidden in the mountains of the Caucasus. The Basayev phenomenon could be explained as a case of "the acculturated native who rebels", an expression first coined by the late Patricia Crone (2012) to refer to a person hailing from a politically subordinate culture who is living in the society of a politically dominant culture and who finds that his ancestral roots are incompatible with the society in which he was born, but against which he now takes political action. Born in the Soviet Republic of Chechnya, Basayev graduated from Soviet schools and served in the Soviet army for two years. With the political crisis of 1991 that led to the collapse of the Soviet Union, Basayev's life took a major turn: he became the most influential leader of a militant Islamic radical group that pursued the creation of an independent Chechen Islamic Republic. Many have argued that the struggle between Putin and Basayev in fact represents a confrontation between Russia and its Muslim citizens, a confrontation which is deep seated in the history of the Tsarist empire and the Soviet Union. Indeed, many have assumed that Muslims have always regarded Moscow as their entrenched enemy for two major reasons: the first is that the house of the Romanovs, like any other colonial empire, conquered lands inhabited by Muslims and denied these Muslims scope for integration unless they acculturated themselves to the Russian society. The second reason is that after the fall of the Russian empire, the Soviet Union waged a war against religions, including Islam, in order to create an atheist society, that is, a society deprived of gods, saints, and spirits. So, according to public opinion, Muslims in Russia have long suffered the oppression of both colonialism (under the guise of the Russian empire) and militant atheism (the USSR).

But one wonders whether it is helpful to frame centuries of relationships between Muslims and Russia only in terms of confrontation, the latter being an idea premised solely on cultural difference, and one which has gained currency especially among disgruntled Russian nationalists (Pomerantsev 2013). My primary concern here is to point out that the situation is far more complex and that for various reasons Muslims could and did feel at home under the rule of the tsars and the Soviets, an idea which has been at the centre of heated debates among Muslim jurists since the seventeenth century (Ross 2020, 23–27; Kemper 2015). In this respect, in order to understand better the relationship between Russia's Muslims and the Kremlin today, it is essential to understand how such a relationship is being explained in Russia at present. Indeed, the time has come to reflect on the fact that under the current government, the public discourse is dominated by an apologetic narrative which presents the history of Islam across the early modern and modern period as one of toleration and benevolence (Rubleva 2023); and the vast majority of Russian Muslims identify with such a narrative.

We can explain the success of this kind of narrative, which presents Russia as a benevolent confessional state, in light of several broad observations. First, imperial Russia's Muslim population was not marginal to the greater Islamic world. By the end of the 18th century, Russia embraced a variety of diverse communities ranging from the Volga River to the Ural Mountains, and Siberia to the Kazakh steppe, Crimea, and the Caucasus. In other words, Russia's Muslims stood at the confluence of multiple cultures and political spheres. They occupied an immense area, which represented the central and northern sections of what once was the Mongol empire, from which they inherited specific forms of governance and cultural practices. Secondly, the Muslim-majority regions of the Russian empire belonged to a cultural area in which Arabic, Persian, and Turkic all functioned as languages of learned communication which enabled elites to transcend regional differences. Indeed, all three languages were employed to facilitate the circulation of Islamic knowledge from the Volga River to the Taklamakan Desert. Thirdly, the Russian empire included important cultural nodes facilitating scholarly traffic within the wider network of global Islamic education. From the mid-1600s to the 1910s, generations of Muslims coming from the Middle Volga and Siberia travelled to institutes of Islamic higher education (*madrasas*) in Central Asia and in the Caucasus. In addition, the Muslim-majority lands ruled by Russia by the late 19th century included the homeland of some of the most prominent scholars in the history of Islam: transmitters of Prophetic traditions, families of jurists, Sufi masters. Ultimately, Muslims found a home in the Russian empire because the state developed institutional arrangements to engage productively with Islam. What I have in mind is that under the rule of Catherine II, the Tsarist authorities established the Mohammedan Ecclesiastical Board, an institution conceived to function as a "Church" for Islam and whose personnel claimed legal and moral authority over other scholars of Islam within the empire. Designed to appoint and control religious personnel across some of the Muslim-majority regions of the empire, it functioned as a Muslim counterpart to the Holy Synod, the body created by Peter the Great earlier in the century to subordinate the Russian Orthodox Church to the state. As we shall see, this institution had lasting consequences for the history of Islam in Russia until today.

The Mohammedan Ecclesiastical Board represented a modern appellate system organised around a simple hierarchy: at the top there was a jurist called the mufti; below the mufti there was a panel of three judges (*qadis*); and at the bottom of the pyramid there was a community of laymen scholars bearing the title of imam and mullahs who operated at the village level. The top tier of the assembly had power of cassation and could therefore overturn the judgments issued by the qadis. Mullahs and imams could only hear disputes orally. They were tasked, nonetheless, with important functions: they had to keep birth, marriage and death registers. They therefore supplied bureaucratic services, and their record-keeping activities could serve the state for purposes of supervision and accountability (Crews 2003).

To sum up, the establishment of the Mohammedan Ecclesiastical Board was a way for the Tsarist regime to create a class of intermediaries who would oversee legal affairs among Muslims on behalf of the state. In this way, the Russian empire attempted to secure stability and control Islam by inviting Muslims to cooperate with the state in the process of defining what it was to be a Muslim. Such a synthesis, as articulated by the generations of scholars who have told this story, of course reflects only a rather narrow approach to the history of the Muslim communities, for one should confer equal historical significance on episodes of violence, forced resettlements, ethnic cleansing and exile which affected Muslims in Russia (Hamed-Troyanski 2024). While I recognise that such stories do not carry much weight under Putin's regime, it is important to remind ourselves that, especially in the nineteenth century, the Russian empire was as Islamophobic as any other colonial empire.

As we move now to the Soviet period, one is tempted to ask whether Islam in the USSR can indeed be a subject of historical inquiry. And this, of course, would be an entirely legitimate question, for we have learnt in the past to think of the USSR as an atheist space where religion barely survived radical policies of modernisation and social engineering. We have been accustomed, for example, to think of Bolshevism as an iconoclastic, destructive movement, and there are countless examples of violent attacks against mosques and murders of Muslim clergy occurring in the 1920s and 1930s. There is definitely no doubt that the USSR was a bulldozer state in a fashion which is only comparable to what China is doing today against its Muslim minority in Xinjiang or what the Serbs did in Kosovo and Bosnia-Herzegovina in the 1990s.

However, it may come as a surprise, but the Soviet state did have institutions of its own to administer believers and religiosity. In fact, in 1917 the USSR was home to different religions including Islam. Not only did the USSR inherit millions of Muslims from the Tsarist empire, but it also relied on the imperial model first created under Catherine II, that is the Mohammedan Ecclesiastical Board. I will come back to this later. In the year 1943, after the Battle of Stalingrad, the Soviet Union had already incurred millions of casualties among the military and the civilians, and Stalin was hard-pressed to mobilise indigenous forces in the war against Nazi Germany. It was at that point that he realised that the Muslims inhabiting the Soviet Union could become a major resource for military conscription. It was the beginning of Stalin's policy of institutionalisation of Islam within the heart of the Soviet state. I put special emphasis on the year 1943, because it is in that context that we can explain why Stalin established various spiritual boards of the Muslims (*muftiates*). The muftiates' mission was to control Muslims according to a model designed more than 150 years earlier in the Tsarist empire. Indeed, it was very similar to the Mohammedan Ecclesiastical Board: it was headed by a mufti, who was flanked by a cohort of scholars who assisted him in various tasks ranging from the writing of sermons to be read out in congregational mosques on Fridays to collecting sensitive data for the KGB. The institution had national branches, and it was at the centre of a web of mosques, whose functioning depended on a registration procedure (Tasar 2017).

Historians have explained that the creation of muftiates was an instrument that Stalin could use to normalise

Muslim-state relations and to stir a feeling of patriotism among the Muslim population during the Second World War. Indeed, in the context of the war muftiates also functioned as mouthpieces of the one-party state. It is telling that Soviet muftis issued fatwas explaining that the war against the Third Reich had to be considered a *jihād* and that conscription into the Red Army represented a religious obligation which fell on all Muslims of the USSR (Eden 2016). Seen from this perspective, the last move by the current Grand Mufti of Chechnya pronouncing a fatwa in favour of the ongoing war in Ukraine is, in fact, a well-trodden path.

But muftiates existed until 1991, so how should we explain their existence beyond the immediate purposes of military mobilisation? From the perspective of Soviet bureaucrats, muftiates had to serve the surveillance apparatus. At the heart of this strategy was the system of *registration*. To open a mosque, a Muslim community would need to be registered with the government. "On paper, it was a brilliant system:" writes Jeff Eden, "'patriotic,' state-supported imams would serve simultaneously as 'religious clergy' and as informants for the regime, while local religious communities were surveilled by non-Muslim Soviet agents" (Eden 2021, 135). There is little doubt that over time the network of the muftiates led to the formation of an Islamic nomenklatura of sorts, which many Muslims in the USSR regarded with suspicion and some openly criticised (Sartori 2024). However, we cannot stress this enough: muftiates represent one of the institutions of the Soviet state which outlived the process of institutional reforms of the 1990s. Most importantly, the system of the Soviet muftiates is still operating not only in the Russian Federation but also in the Muslim-majority successor countries to the USSR.

In the first days of the war of aggression against Ukraine, many questioned how Russia could mobilise Muslims into a holy war. To approach this question solely from a utilitarian point of view would necessarily lead to ignoring the extent to which many non-Orthodox and non-Slavic communities feel themselves at home in Russia and identify with Putin's call for action to defend Russia's spiritual values, not only people of Orthodox derivation, but also those with an Islamic, Buddhist, and animistic background.

The institutionalisation of religion, and especially Islam, first in the Russian empire and then in the USSR, has been conducive to creating what with some latitude can be termed a pact of steel between the state and religiously-minded communities beyond the boundaries of Orthodoxy. This can best be appreciated by observing how not only clerics, but also laymen in Russia today have embraced and reify an apologetic narrative whereby Catherine II's policies of toleration brought about an Islamic renaissance in the heart of Eurasia (Bustanov 2016). And one of the objectives of current propaganda under Putin's regime is to reify the idea of that "enlightened" spirit. For a country like the Russian Federation, which has been plagued by a demographic crisis generated by a falling birth rate since the 1990s, non-Orthodox religious communities therefore represent a significant resource for the current war in Ukraine. The scope of such a resource will not only reflect the capacity of the state to remunerate families for their war effort, but it will also be contingent on the ability of state authorities to offer something valuable in the ideological marketplace of religion.

BIBLIOGRAPHY

Bustanov, A. (2016) Obraz Èkateriny II i ideia s "vozrozhdeniem" iavliaiutsia rezul'tatom kakogo to zakulisnogo kompromissa. V real'noe vremia. 20 April 2016. https://m.realnoevremya.ru/articles/29225 (Last accessed 12 February 2025).

Crews, R. (2003) Empire and the Confessional State: Islam and Religious Politics in Nineteenth-Century Russia, *American History Review* 108, 50–83.

Crone, P. (2012) The Acculturated Native Who Rebels: Nativists, Nationalists, and Western-Born Jihadists in Historical Perspective (Lecture held at the Institute of Advanced Studies, Princeton. 26 April 2012). https://www.ias.edu/press-releases/patricia-crone-places-nativists-nationalists-and-western-born-jihadists-historical (Last accessed 12 February 2025).

Dijskra, Z. (2022) Loyalty or Resistance to Moscow? A Difficult Dilemma for Russian Orthodox Churches, *EARS Newsletter*. 11 April 2022. https://europeanacademyofreligionandsociety.com/news/loyalty-or-resistance-to-moscow-a-difficult-dilemma-for-russian-orthodox-churches/ (Last accessed 12 February 2025).

Eden, J. (2016) A Soviet Jihad against Hitler: Ishan Babakhan Calls Central Asian Muslims to War, *Journal of the Economic and Social History of the Orient* 59, 237–264.

Eden, J. (2021) *God Save the USSR*. Oxford: Oxford University Press.

Hamed-Troyanski, V. (2024) *Empire of Refugees: North Caucasian Muslims and the Late Ottoman State*. Stanford: Stanford University Press.

Holl-Allen, G. (2023) Desperate Putin Sends Religious Icon to Front Line to Boost Morale. *The Telegraph*. 29 May 2023.

Kemper, M. (2015) Imperial Russia as Dar al-Islam? Nineteenth-Century Debates on Ijtihad and Taqlid among the Volga Tatars, *Encounters* 6, 95–124.

The Moscow Times (2019) Kremlin is Spending $43M to Renovate Imperial Mansion for Orthodox Patriarch, Media Reports. *The Moscow Times*. 21 May 2019. https://www.themoscowtimes.com/2019/05/21/kremlin-is-spending-43-million-renovate-imperial-mansion-orthodox-patriarch-a65667 (Last accessed 12 February 2025).

Muhammad, H. H. and Soliev, N. (2023) Examining Theological Justifications for Kadyrovite Chechens Fighting in Ukraine. 28 March 2023. https://www.hudson.org/examining-theological-justifications-kadyrovite-chechens-fighting-ukraine (Last accessed 12 February 2025).

Pomerantsev, P. (2013) Russia for Russians, *The London Review of Books Blog*. 5 November 2013. https://www.lrb.co.uk/blog/2013/november/russia-for-russians (Last accessed 12 February 2025).

Ross, D. (2020) *Tatar Empire: Kazan's Muslims and the Making of Imperial Russia*. Bloomington, IN: Indiana University Press.

Rubleva, T. (2023) Kak Èkaterina II zalozhila osnovy religioznoy tolerantnosti? *Radio MIR*. 30 June 2023. https://mir24.tv/articles/16557306/kak-ekaterina-ii-zalozhila-osnovy-religioznoi-tolerantnosti (Last accessed 12 February 2025).

Sartori, P. (2024) *A Soviet Sultanate: Islam in Socialist Uzbekistan*, 1943–1991. Vienna: Austrian Academy of Sciences Press.

Tasar, E. (2017) *Soviet and Muslim: The Institutionalization of Islam in Central Asia*. Oxford: Oxford University Press.

Whalen, J. (2022) Russian Orthodox Leader Backs War in Ukraine, Divides Faith, *The Washington Post*. 18 April 2022. https://www.washingtonpost.com/world/2022/04/18/russian-orthodox-church-ukraine-war/ (Last accessed 12 February 2025).

ISLAM IN RUSSIA'S DOMESTIC AND FOREIGN POLICY AFTER 2022

GULNAZ SIBGATULLINA

Gulnaz Sibgatullina is an assistant professor at the University of Amsterdam in the Netherlands. Her research focuses on Islam in Europe, contemporary Islamic thought, state-church relations, and minority issues in Russia.

Contemporary Russia's identity as a multi-ethnic and multi-religious state has deep historical roots, shaped by a colonial legacy extending back to the 16th century. A critical juncture in this history was the 1552 annexation of the Kazan Khanate, a Muslim state that is a predecessor of today's Republic of Tatarstan, one of Russia's Muslim republics. This event marked the beginning of Russia's transformation into an empire that would expand eastward into Siberia and southward into the Caucasus and Central Asia, incorporating numerous indigenous peoples along the way.

Unlike Western European empires, where Muslim populations often resided in overseas colonies, Muslim communities in Russia have long been an integral part of its contiguous territories. Muslims have not only been present in remote regions but also in major trade and cultural hubs, forming a visible and significant minority within Russia. Their enduring presence has posed challenges to Russian imperial and, later, Soviet governments, which, from the outset, needed to address the complexities of governing a large, non-Christian population within its borders. The tsars' methods of consolidating loyalty among Muslim populations included a mix of coercion, co-optation, displacement, extermination, terror, cultural assimilation, and selective religious toleration (Geraci 2001; Crews 2006; Campbell 2015). These tactics persisted, albeit adapted, through the Soviet era (Tasar 2017; Sartori 2024). The challenges associated with governing Muslim populations also remained salient in Russia after the fall of the Soviet Union in 1991, as evidenced by the protracted Chechen conflicts of the 1990s and early 2000s. However, besides the need to find means to govern ethnically, culturally, and religiously diverse communities brought together under the umbrella term of "Muslim", having this population within the territories of the empire has also provided the imperial centre with some strategic benefits. Beyond extracting resources, knowledge, and cultural artefacts from these communities, the Russian Empire and, later, the Soviet Union leveraged the symbolic power of its Muslim populations. This dynamic was especially prominent during the Cold War, when Soviet Muslim republics were highlighted in Soviet propaganda aimed at aligning with anti-colonial movements in the Third World (Kirasirova 2011; Kalinovsky 2013). By presenting itself as a state inclusive of Muslim-majority regions, the Soviet Union sought to attract decolonising nations in Africa, Asia, and the Middle East. In the post-Soviet era, Russia has continued to reposition Islam from a potential liability to a strategic asset.

In this essay, which centres on the role of Islam in Russia's contemporary, particularly post-2022, foreign and domestic policies, I argue that not only the Russian Orthodox Church but also Islamic institutions facilitate the advancement of Russia's illiberal and conservative agenda. Islamic institutions contribute to the legitimacy of the current Russian regime domestically, mirroring the Orthodox Church's efforts to maintain a religious influence in society by promoting traditional family values and conservative gender norms. Internationally, Kremlin-aligned Islamic leaders serve as intermediaries, strengthening Russia's diplomatic relations with Muslim-majority nations in what is commonly, albeit not unproblematically, known as the "Global South".

ISLAMIC IDEOLOGICAL ENTREPRENEURS

In a contemporary era marked by fluid identities and shifting boundaries of social belonging, the limitations of terms like "Muslim" or "Islam" in fully capturing complex realities have been particularly evident (Brubaker 2013). References to "Russia's Muslims" typically denote a religious minority that comprises a rich mosaic of ethnic communities, including Bashkir, Uzbek, Tatar, and Chechen peoples. Some of these groups can be considered indigenous to Russian territories, though even within this category, one will find related but different experiences of imperial control and integration; while others have emerged in post-Soviet Russia through postcolonial migration from now-independent republics in Central Asia.

The colonial past partly explains why the "Muslim question" in Russia has been intrinsically linked to minority ethnic nationalism since at least the 19th century. This connection has, at times, manifested in what, depending on one's perspective, can be called a "struggle for independence" or "separatism", creating tension between the centre and Muslim-majority regions throughout Russian history. Many contemporary observers continue to emphasise ethnic-religious minority nationalism, anticipating that the interplay of these identities in the aftermath of the 2022 invasion will destabilise Moscow's control over the subjects of the Federation. However, the intersections of religious, ethnic, and particularly civilisational and class identities have not remained static; rather, they have evolved significantly over the past 30 post-Soviet years (Mitrokhin 2023). This transformation happened, as during the post-Soviet period, the Kremlin has never functioned as a totalitarian monolith. Instead, it has fostered a variety of ideological ecosystems (Laruelle 2017b) led by "ideological entrepreneurs", individuals who took advantage of a degree of ideological latitude before state-imposed red lines became rigid. Although the space for ideological manoeuvring has narrowed considerably over the past decade, particularly since 2022, the preceding period of relative flexibility allowed certain ideological entrepreneurs to ascend to influential positions. Within the realm of Islam, these entrepreneurs have contributed to the redefinition of Islam not as an opposing force to the Kremlin's ideological course but as one that shares its goals. The actors can be categorised into two main groups, each operating with distinct Muslim credentials.

The first type is closely associated with the system of muftiates. To put it in a slightly oversimplified manner, a muftiate is a Muslim analogue of the Russian Orthodox Church, in the sense of a body that responds to the needs of its religious community and operates as a mediator between the state and the communities. Yet, unlike the Russian Orthodox Church, which is a more or less unified, hierarchical body, there is not one but multiple muftiates. Part of the reason for the existing pluralism is the variation within Russia's Muslim space—no single body can claim to represent the existing diversity of secular, Sufi, variations of Sunni, and Shi'a Muslims. Another reason, particularly characteristic of the post-Soviet period, is the competition for power and authority among the numerous muftiates, which has resulted in further fragmentation (Bekkin 2020).

In my previous work, I have argued that post-Soviet muftiates often adopt discursive strategies akin to those of the Orthodox Church, utilising similar language to discuss religious matters. This approach serves practical purposes, allowing muftiates to signal loyalty towards the state and, consequently, to secure political and financial support. However, the implications of this strategy are also theological. By employing Russian terms for "God" and "prayer" that mirror Orthodox Christian usage, the ideological content shared between Islam and Orthodox Christianity blurs the distinctions between the two faiths at the official level (Sibgatullina 2020). This does not imply an imminent threat of Christianisation for Russia's Muslims; distinct rituals and private practices continue to be governed by Islamic traditions. Nevertheless, it suggests that in the public sphere, the state increasingly promotes a unified conservative "Abrahamism", potentially encompassing various Islamic and Christian denominations under a single ideological framework (Sibgatullina 2024). Despite a degree of recognition afforded to Islam by the state, the relationship between Orthodox Christianity and Islam within this "Abrahamism" is far from equal, as Islamic ideological entrepreneurs operate under the heavy shadow of the Orthodox Church.

The second group of ideological entrepreneurs comprises Muslim leaders closely aligned with secular power structures, with Ramzan Kadyrov, the head of Chechnya, as a prominent example. Following the assassination of his father, Akhmad Kadyrov, in

2004, Ramzan ascended to power, establishing an authoritarian regime within the Chechen Republic characterised by political repression, kidnappings, and torture of opponents. Kadyrov's ideological stance has been particularly impactful. He has reframed Chechen nationalism—historically anti-colonial and separatist—into a pro-Russian patriotism that positions Chechens as integral to Russia's success (Laruelle 2017a). This reconfiguration legitimises puritanical, hierarchical, and hyper-masculine forms of Islam within Russia, presenting an alternative to European models of Islamic representation that emphasise cultural liberalisation and secularisation. Kadyrov gained particular visibility in the early stages of the large-scale invasion of Ukraine, as his forces, known as the "Kadyrovtsy", claimed front-line roles and broadcasted hypermasculine Islamic religiosity via social media (Mirovalev 2022). Although the actual extent of the Kadyrovtsy's involvement in regular Russian army operations has been disputed, their actions and public reactions to them have demonstrated an uneasy coexistence of ultra-patriotism and deeply rooted Islamophobic sentiments within the broader Russian society. In addition to catering to domestic audiences, Kadyrov's connections with Gulf states have proven strategically advantageous on the international stage. These connections have provided Russian officials with additional diplomatic channels and the potential to strengthen Russia's alliances within the Muslim world (Laruelle 2022).

IDEOLOGICAL FOUNDATIONS OF RUSSIA'S APPEAL: THE ROLE OF MUSLIM LEADERS

In crafting an appealing narrative for both domestic and international audiences, these Muslim ideological entrepreneurs have contributed to the backbone of Russia's state ideology, which is grounded in three distinct but interconnected tenets: a critique of liberal secularism, the advocacy of traditional values, and a portrayal of Russia as a unique model of inclusive citizenship. Each of these aspects reinforces Russia's positioning as an alternative to Western liberalism, supporting the Kremlin's arguments for the diversity of civilisations and multipolarity in the global political arena (Gamburd 2024). This approach has enabled Russia to align with conservative allies worldwide, especially religious actors—both Christian and Islamic—who challenge the dominance of liberal hegemony on both local and international stages.

1. *Critique of Liberal Secularism.* Muslim leaders have been important for Russia's ideological critique of liberalism, particularly targeting secularism. Within this framework, secularism's relegation of religion to the private sphere is seen as fostering individualism, weakening societal norms, and promoting moral decay. From this perspective, the West's diminishing emphasis on spiritual values is portrayed as leading to liberalism's hollow promise of superficial consumer gratification. Within the Russian ideological narrative, Christianity—and, by extension, Islam—are portrayed as the essential societal pillars that counteract this moral decay. The promotion of a unified conservative ideology that merges Christian and Islamic values increasingly blurs the boundaries not only between the two religious systems but also between the secular and religious nature of the Russian state. Religion has been functioning not simply as a cultural or ethical backdrop but as a state-supported ideological framework. Domestically, this ideo-

logical synthesis allows the state—still nominally secular, though with a growing explicit Orthodox Christian identity following the 2020 Constitutional Amendments (Stoeckl 2020)—to champion at low cost certain Muslim interests, thereby contributing to its pro-Muslim international image. For example, the state has allowed massive protests against Western cartoons depicting the Prophet Muhammad, positioning itself if not as a defender, then at least as tolerant of Muslim sensitivities (VOA 2015). On the international stage, Russia-linked actors frame their stance as a defence of religious communities against Western secular tendencies to confine religion strictly to the private sphere. While this rhetoric currently focuses primarily on Orthodox Christian groups (Kłyszcz 2024), it has the potential to extend to Muslim communities, emphasising a shared resistance to perceived Western encroachments on religious and cultural values. By tapping into a growing anti-Western sentiment, this approach finds resonance across diverse audiences in the "Global South"—from Uganda to Indonesia—where the historical legacy of Western secularism is often viewed as disruptive to traditional religious practices and identities.

2. *Advocacy for Traditional Values*. The second ideological foundation involves a strong emphasis on so-called "traditional values", focusing on conservative gender roles and the preservation of the heterosexual nuclear family as the core of society. Muslim intellectuals within Russia have significantly contributed to shaping a version of conservative Islam that supports this narrative while aligning with the country's non-Muslim governance (Sibgatullina 2023). This synthesis of religious and secular nationalism positions conservative Islam as a partner rather than an antagonist to the state, allowing for a shared platform of values that can transcend religious divides within Russian society. This appeal to traditional values resonates with a domestic Muslim audience that, like other parts of Russian society, has experienced profound social and economic upheavals following the Soviet Union's dissolution. The neoliberal transition and resulting social disintegration fostered a sense of ressentiment, channelled into a pervasive distrust of Western influences, which are perceived as instruments of cultural and ideological control (Sharafutdinova 2016). Coupled with this is a general climate of societal instability that further strengthens the desire to preserve elements of society that are seen as stable and functional. On the global stage, Russia leverages this ideological stance to position itself as a defender of traditional values amid global culture wars. Its support for illiberal actors worldwide, both Muslim and Christian, broadens its appeal to pro-family, pro-religion networks that are seeking alternatives to Western liberalism. This has facilitated alliances with ideologically diverse groups, including the Christian Right in the United States and Islamic leaders within the United Nations (Stoeckl and Uzlaner 2022).

3. *Representation of an Inclusive Model of Citizenship*. The third ideological pillar of Russia's state rhetoric centres on its portrayal as a nation with an inclusive model of citizenship that genuinely embraces Muslim minorities—a model Russia claims is in stark contrast to Western Europe's approach. Unlike Western European countries, which have relatively recent histories of integrating Muslim migrants from former colonies, Russia emphasises its centuries-old experience governing a wide array of ethnic and religious groups, a legacy of both its imperial and Soviet past. This historical narrative is used

to construct an image of "harmony" and "peaceful coexistence" between Muslims and non-Muslims within Russia (e.g. Galeeva 2024).

Through this lens, Russia positions itself internationally against former European empires, like France and England, which face criticism for their institutional racism and challenges in integrating postcolonial migrants. By presenting itself as a nation where imperial hierarchies were either dismantled or, in some interpretations, never formally existed, Moscow taps into Soviet anti-imperialist narratives that continue to resonate with post-colonial societies worldwide (Young 2024). Domestically, however, this narrative has been difficult to uphold. Under President Vladimir Putin's leadership, Moscow has intensified crackdowns on ethnic and religious minority rights. The frequent surveillance, marginalisation, and assimilationist pressures on certain ethnic and religious communities—particularly Muslims—reveal a disconnect between Russia's idealised self-image and its current policies.

DOMESTIC CHALLENGES

Although ideologically beneficial, Moscow's strategy of co-opting Islamic leaders carries significant risks. Over the past two decades, the Kremlin has viewed ethnic identity within minority groups as a greater threat to internal stability than religious identity, which it perceives as more manageable within carefully structured frameworks. This approach has resulted in a bifurcation of Islamic practice into categories like "traditional" versus "Salafi" and "good" versus "bad", with strict penalties for deviations from officially sanctioned forms (Aitamurto 2016). Consequently, Moscow has permitted the promotion and celebration of certain "traditional" religious aspects of ethnic minority identities, even in regions where ethnic minority identity itself is seen as threatening. For instance, in Tatarstan the state permits celebrations of Islamic heritage, such as anniversaries of the region's adoption of Islam (Kashapov 2022). In contrast, commemorations of Tatarstan's historical incorporation into the Russian state are prohibited (Meduza 2024). This emphasis on the religious rather than ethnic identity of minorities within Russia first of all obscures the diversity that exists among Muslim communities. By framing Muslims as a homogeneous group, this rhetoric contributes to the essentialisation of "Muslimness" and inadvertently fuels Islamophobic currents within Russian society (Calderone and Aziz 2024). As distinctions between Uzbek and Chechen Muslim identities, for instance, are blurred in the public eye, and anxieties about the growing number of Muslims in Russia and perceived "Islamisation" have found fertile ground. This generalised view not only intensifies inter-ethnic tensions but also exacerbates xenophobia, directed both at "foreign" migrant workers and at "local" Muslims who are citizens of the Russian Federation. Moreover, as the centre-region relationship in Russia becomes increasingly defined by religious rather than ethnic categories, it also reshapes local expressions of discontent. Muslim communities—both migrant and indigenous—avoid direct confrontations with state authority, an approach made even more necessary by the severe criminalisation of dissent in contemporary Russia. Instead, these communities often prioritise religious/personal over secular/official, resulting in the formation of "parallel" societies. These "halal spaces" (Kaliszewska 2020) operate largely outside the state's direct control, where subtle and indirect forms of resistance to state authority emerge.

Since February 2022, the gap between official religious leadership—both Muslim and Orthodox—and broader community sentiment has become increasingly evident. Some Muslim leaders have aligned closely with the Kremlin, framing participation in the war as a religious duty (Sibgatullina 2022). However, the Russia-Ukraine war has disproportionately affected minority communities, especially in its early stages, when Muslim men were drafted at higher rates (Lenton 2022). In subsequent phases, economic necessity has driven others to volunteer, underscoring the intersection of ethnicity, class, and religion in ways that reveal persistent inequalities across ethnic and socioeconomic divides (Idel.Realii 2024). The Kremlin's challenges are further complicated by the ongoing threat of Islamist groups within Russia, as evidenced by the recent terrorist attack in Moscow in March 2024. While the authorities perceive the growing visibility of Russia's Muslim demographic as strategically advantageous—both in terms of attracting labour and in projecting influence abroad—they remain wary of the potential volatility this visibility can bring. Moscow's approach thus continues to involve a balancing act: leveraging the benefits of a cohesive Muslim presence while containing the inter-ethnic and inter-religious tensions it might provoke.

FOREIGN POLICY CHALLENGES

Russia's large-scale invasion of Ukraine in 2022 elicited a swift response from the West, characterised by extensive sanctions and diplomatic efforts aimed at isolating Russia in the global political and economic landscape. In reaction to this, Moscow has intensified a pre-existing strategy—already evident before and during the COVID-19 pandemic—focused on reinforcing its presence and influence within the "Global South" (e.g. Audinet and Limonier 2022). Several interrelated factors have facilitated this re-engagement: the reluctance of many "Global South" nations to publicly condemn Russia's actions, widespread critiques among them of Western international governance, for instance, in vaccine distribution and aid strategies, and a certain nostalgia for the Soviet Union's anti-colonial, leftist solidarity agenda (Sabanadze 2024).

Although Russia's direct economic and political sway over Muslim-majority countries is relatively constrained, its focused soft power initiatives are difficult to ignore. While strategic media outreach through channels such as RT and Sputnik Arabic (Styszyński 2023) has helped shape its image, high-profile international events have bolstered ties with these countries. For example, in May 2024, Kazan—the capital of Tatarstan—hosted the Russia-Islamic World Forum, designed as an Islamic counterpart to the St. Petersburg International Economic Forum. Targeting member nations of the Organisation of Islamic Cooperation, this gathering promoted Russia's integration into halal trade and tourism networks, signalling a pragmatic alignment with economic interests across the Muslim world (KazanForum 2024). The October 2024 BRICS summit that also took place in Kazan further demonstrated Russia's adeptness at offsetting global isolation by strengthening ties with influential states in the Islamic world. Enhanced cooperation with Iran—and a more cautious engagement with Saudi

Arabia—supports the Kremlin's narrative of "multipolarity" in global politics, echoing shared scepticism of Western dominance (Aydıntaşbaş et al. 2024). However, while Russia symbolically champions a challenge to Western liberal hegemony, it offers little ideological depth to Muslim-majority countries, which themselves face internal disunity and divergent political agendas, particularly evident in the ongoing Israel-Palestine conflict and broader regional tensions. As a result, their cooperation with Russia mirrors Cold War dynamics, remaining primarily pragmatic but infused with a degree of affinity for belonging to the "Rest" rather than the West.

This current state of affairs reflects a historical pattern in which Russia strategically employs its "Muslim nature" as part of its broader narrative to distinguish itself from "white Christian Europe". Historically, Russia's Muslim communities, particularly those of Turkic descent, have been integral to its self-image as a unique Eurasian civilisation that harmonises Eastern and Western elements (Laruelle 2008). Presently, Russia's outward expression of Muslim-friendliness coexists with strict control over religious expression and freedoms domestically, particularly among its Muslim population. This dualistic approach—presenting a façade of inclusivity on the international stage while enforcing repressive governance domestically—reveals an underlying tension in the Kremlin's policies, leaving them vulnerable to international critique and fuelling potential discontent within Russia.

RELIGIOUS SOFT POWER

Following periods of containment and securitisation, the 2020s have witnessed Islam, still a marginalised minority religion in Russia, gain heightened visibility within the country's ideological framework. On the international stage, highly publicised collaborations between the Kremlin and Islamic institutions or states signify a pragmatic, politically expedient alignment rather than a deeply rooted ideological affinity. Domestically, however, Islamic leaders contribute—though to a far lesser degree than their Russian Orthodox counterparts—to the construction of a cohesive ideological narrative and moral framework. The ongoing war may further alter these dynamics, potentially elevating into a more prominent ideological role those Islamic leaders who are capable of intertwining patriotism and Russian nationalism with Islamic identity. This ideological strategy is fundamentally contingent on the demonstration of loyalty to the state by Muslim communities. This conditional acceptance underscores a complex relationship in which the state leverages religious identities to bolster its own authority while simultaneously imposing strict limits on religious expression and community autonomy. Although the ethnic identities of these Muslim communities have been consistently downplayed, the context of war risks reigniting discussions of nationalism: both ethnic minority nationalism, which demands greater political autonomy, and Russian nationalism, which could exacerbate xenophobic and inter-ethnic tensions.

Regardless of future developments, the visibility of Islam within Russia's domestic and foreign policies underscores the rising importance of religion in today's geopolitical landscape, signalling the re-emergence of religion as a political challenge to secular liberalism. The strategic adoption of religion by influential states—including Russia, Turkey, and China

(Mandaville 2023)—reflects a broadening political role for religious actors and their international networks. This shift suggests a broader trend, extending beyond Russia, in which religion serves not only as a basis for national culture or individual identity but also as a powerful instrument used by otherwise secular states for political mobilisation and influence.

BIBLIOGRAPHY

Aitamurto, K. (2016) The Approved and the Disapproved Islam in Russia, *Religion, Politics and Nation-Building in Post-Communist Countries*, edited by G. Simons and D. Westerlund. London: Routledge, 99–116.

Audinet, M. and Limonier, K. (2022) Le dispositif d'influence informationnelle de la Russie en Afrique subsaharienne francophone: un écosystème flexible et composite, *Questions de communication* 41 (June), 129–48.

Aydıntaşbaş, A. et al. (2024) What Can We Expect from the 2024 BRICS Summit?, *Brookings*. 21 October 2024. https://www.brookings.edu/articles/what-can-we-expect-from-the-2024-brics-summit/ (Last accessed 12 February 2025).

Bekkin, R. (2020) *People of Reliable Loyalty… : Muftiates and the State in Modern Russia*. PhD dissertation, Södertörn University.

Brubaker, R. (2013) Categories of Analysis and Categories of Practice: A Note on the Study of Muslims in European Countries of Immigration, *Ethnic and Racial Studies* 36 (1), 1–8.

Calderone, S. and Aziz, S. F. (2024) Islamophobia in Russia: Ethnicity, Migration, and National Security, *Global Islamophobia and the Rise of Populism*, edited by S. F. Aziz and J. L. Esposito. Oxford University Press. Pre-publication: https://doi.org/10.1093/oso/9780197648995.003.0009.

Campbell, E. I. (2015) *The Muslim Question and Russian Imperial Governance*. Bloomington, IN: Indiana University Press.

Crews, R. D. (2006) *For Prophet and Tsar: Islam and Empire in Russia and Central Asia*. Cambridge, MA: Harvard University Press.

Galeeva, D. (2024) *Islam in Russia: Formations of Tolerance*. New York, NY: Routledge.

Gamburd, A. (2024) Russian Narrative: Civilizationism and Multipolarity, *Harvard International Review*. 29 May 2024. https://hir.harvard.edu/russian-narrative-constitutional-amendments-civilizationism-and-multipolarity/ (Last accessed 12 February 2025).

Geraci, R. (2001) *Window on the East: National and Imperial Identities in Late Tsarist Russia*. Ithaca, NY: Cornell University Press.

Idel.Realii (2024) Voina s Ukrainoi: pogibshie iz Povolzh'ia, *Radio Free Europe / Radio Liberty*. 2024. https://www.idelreal.org/a/voyna-s-ukrainoy-pogibshie-iz-povolzhya/31916592.html (Last accessed 12 February 2025).

Kalinovsky, A. M. (2013) Not Some British Colony in Africa: The Politics of Decolonization and Modernization in Soviet Central Asia, 1955-1964, *Ab Imperio* 2013 (2), 191–222.

Kaliszewska, I. (2020) Halal Landscapes of Dagestani Entrepreneurs in Makhachkala, *Ethnicities* 20 (4), 708–30.

Kashapov, R. (2022) The 1100th Anniversary of Adoption of Islam by Volga Bulgaria in Tatarstan, *Real'noe Vremia*. 7 January 2022. https://realnoevremya.com/articles/6101-the-1100th-anniversary-of-adoption-of-islam-by-volga-bulgaria-in-tatarstan (Last accessed 12 February 2025).

KazanForum (2024) About Forum, Russia - Islamic World: KazanForum. https://kazanforum.ru/en/exhibition/about/ (Last accessed 12 February 2025).

Kirasirova, M. (2011) "Sons of Muslims" in Moscow: Soviet Central Asian Mediators to the Foreign East, 1955–1962, *Ab Imperio* 2011 (4), 106–32.

Kłyszcz, I. U. (2024) Russia's Spiritual Expansion in the Global South, *The Russia Program*. 27 May 2024. https://therussiaprogram.org/spiritual_expansion (Last accessed 12 February 2025).

Laruelle, M. (2008) *Russian Eurasianism: An Ideology of Empire*. Washingon, DC: Johns Hopkins University Press.

Laruelle, M. (2017a) Kadyrovism: Hardline Islam as a Tool of the Kremlin?, IFRI Paris Cedex 15. https://www.ifri.org/en/papers/kadyrovism-hardline-islam-tool-kremlin (Last accessed 12 February 2025).

Laruelle, M. (2017b) The Kremlin's Ideological Ecosystems: Equilibrium and Competition, *PonarsEuarasia - Policy Memos*, November. https://www.ponarseurasia.org/memo/kremlins-ideological-ecosystems-equilibrium-and-competition (Last accessed 12 February 2025).

Laruelle, M. (2022) Russia at War and the Islamic World, IFRI, December. https://www.ifri.org/sites/default/files/migrated_files/documents/atoms/files/rnv127_laruelle_ukraine_muslims.pdf (Last accessed 12 February 2025).

Lenton, A. (2022) Who Is Dying for the «Russian World»?, *Riddle Russia*. 26 April 2022. https://ridl.io/who-is-dying-for-the-russian-world/ (Last accessed 12 February 2025).

Mandaville, P. (2023) *The Geopolitics of Religious Soft Power: How States Use Religion in Foreign Policy*. Oxford: Oxford University Press.

Meduza (2024) V Tatarstane zapretili ezhegodnyi miting, *Meduza*. 7 October 2024. https://meduza.io/news/2024/10/07/v-tatarstane-zapretili-ezhegodnyy-miting-v-pamyat-o-pogibshih-pri-oborone-kazani-ot-voysk-ivana-groznogo (Last accessed 12 February 2025).

Mirovalev, M. (2022) The Real Role of Pro-Russian Chechens in Ukraine, *Al Jazeera*. 18 August 2022. https://www.aljazeera.com/news/2022/8/18/the-real-role-of-pro-russian-chechens-in-ukraine (Last accessed 12 February 2025).

Mitrokhin, N. (2023) Where Are Russia's Nationalists in the War Against Ukraine?, *Carnegie Endowment for International Peace*. 7 March 2023. https://carnegieendowment.org/russia-eurasia/politika/2023/02/where-are-russias-nationalists-in-the-war-against-ukraine?lang=en (Last accessed 12 February 2025).

Sabanadze, N. (2024) Russia Is Using the Soviet Playbook in the Global South to Challenge the West – and It Is Working, *Chatham House*. 16 May 2024. https://www.chathamhouse.org/2024/05/russia-using-soviet-playbook-global-south-challenge-west-and-it-working (Last accessed 12 February 2025).

Sartori, P. (2024) *A Soviet Sultanate: Islam in Socialist Uzbekistan (1943-1991)*. Vienna: Austrian Academy of Sciences Press.

Sharafutdinova, G. (2016) Managing National Ressentiment: Morality Politics in Putin's Russia, *Vocabularies of International Relations after the Crisis in Ukraine*, edited by A. Makarychev and A. Yatsyk. London: Ashgate Publishing, 130–51.

Sibgatullina, G. (2020) *Languages of Islam and Christianity in Post-Soviet Russia*. Leiden: Brill Rodopi.

Sibgatullina, G. (2022) Russia's Muslim Leaders on the Invasion of Ukraine: United in a Display of Loyalty, Divided in Competition for Power, *PONARS*. 7 April 2022. https://www.ponarseurasia.org/russias-muslim-leaders-on-the-invasion-of-ukraine-united-in-a-display-of-loyalty-divided-in-competition-for-power/ (Last accessed 12 February 2025).

Sibgatullina, G. (2023) The Muftis and the Myths: Constructing the Russian "Church for Islam", *Problems of Post-Communism*, March, 1–12.

Sibgatullina, G. (2024) Russia's Conservative Religious Consensus: Forging an Illiberal Global Solidarity, *Religion, State and Society* 52 (4), 420–22.

Stoeckl, K. (2020) Russian Orthodoxy and Secularism, *Brill Research Perspectives in Religion and Politics* 1 (2), 1–75. https://doi.org/10.1163/25895850-12340002.

Stoeckl, K. and Uzlaner, D. (2022) *The Moralist International: Russia in the Global Culture Wars*. New York, NY: Fordham University Press.

Styszyński, M. (2023) Arab Context of the Ukraine Conflict in Russia Today Arabic and Sputnik, *Krakowskie Studia Międzynarodowe* XX (1), 121–37.

Tasar, E. (2017) *Soviet and Muslim: The Institutionalization of Islam in Central Asia*. Oxford: Oxford University Press.

VOA (2015) Protest Against Muhammad Caricatures Draws Chechens, *Voice of America*. 19 January 2015. https://www.voanews.com/a/reu-hundreds-of-thousands-protest-in-chechnya-against-prophet-muhammad-cartoons/2604432.html (Last accessed 12 February 2025).

Young, Benjamin R. (2024) Russia Is Riding an Anti-Colonial Wave Across Africa, *Rand Corporation*. 16 September 2024. https://www.rand.org/pubs/commentary/2024/09/russia-is-riding-an-anti-colonial-wave-across-africa.html (Last accessed 12 February 2025).

RELIGION, LAW AND POLITICS FOR A RUSSIA AT WAR[1]

KRISTINA STOECKL

Kristina Stoeckl is a professor of sociology at Luiss (Rome) and previously held a professorship at Innsbruck University. A recipient of an ERC Starting Grant and alumna of the Young Academy of the Austrian Academy of Sciences, her research explores religion, politics, and global culture wars.

INTRODUCTION

In mid-May 2023, the ecclesiastical court of the Russian Orthodox Church defrocked the priest Ioann Koval, aged 45, for changing one word in a prayer that the patriarch of Moscow had issued to all churches in support of Russia's war in Ukraine. The text of the prayer featured the line "Rise up, O Lord, for the help of thy people, and grant us victory by thy power". Koval instead prayed "Rise up, O Lord, for the help of thy people, and grant us peace by thy power" (Chapnin 2023). The priest was denounced by a parishioner for changing the word "victory" to "peace" and was punished for disobedience. Less than two weeks later, Patriarch Kirill suspended Archpriest Leonid Kalinin from his position as head of the Patriarchal Expert Commission for Church Art, Architecture and Restoration and barred him from celebrating mass. The priest, aged 55, had opposed the decision to move the fifteenth-century Icon of the Trinity by Andrey Rublev from its location in the restoration workshop of the Tretyakov Gallery to be placed on public display in Moscow's Cathedral of Christ the Saviour on grounds of concerns over the safety of the artwork. Days before, Russian President

1 This article is a shortened version of: Stoeckl, Kristina, "The Pact of the Old Guard: Religion, Law, and Politics for a Russia at War", Journal of Law and Religion, published online: 1–12 (DOI: https://doi.org/10.1017/jlr.2024.22), 2024 © Cambridge University Press, reproduced with permission.

Vladimir Putin had promised to return the icon, which had been confiscated by the Bolsheviks a century before, to church property (Interfax 2023). These incidents are just two examples of the ideological narrowing within the Russian Orthodox Church since the start of Russia's full-scale war against Ukraine in February 2022.

By unleashing a war against Ukraine, a narrow circle of political and ecclesiastical leaders has decided the fate of Russia and the Russian Orthodox Church. This "old guard" is not only old in age—President Putin aged 70, Patriarch Kirill aged 76, and the former secretary of the Security Council Nikolaj Patrushev aged 71, to name just these three—but it is also steeped in one and the same worldview guided by Soviet revanchism, nationalism, and militarism. The place of religion in this worldview is limited to the church as a provider of ritual and spiritual wrappings for ideology, and as the arc of time that connects the past, present, and future of the Russian nation. The old guard does not have a place for independent religious thinking, as in the examples above, and it follows a logic of authority, control, obedience, and friend-enemy that appears deeply engrained in the Soviet-era security services.

The period under discussion has been amply discussed in academic literature[2] and the analysis in this article does not add new empirics to the field. Instead, it recomposes some of the main axes of interpretation in the light of Russia's war against Ukraine. The argument proceeds in three chronological steps. First, I sketch the beginning and the end of the Russian Orthodox Church's multiple post-Soviet identities based on the experiences of repression, collaboration, dissidence, and emigration from 1991 until roughly 2010. Second, I pick out the most significant legislative and political steps between 2010 and 2021 that have contributed to turning the Russian Orthodox Church into an ally of the autocratic state. Third, I look at Patriarch Kirill's support of Russia's full-scale war against Ukraine since 2022[3] and interpret this self-positioning in the conflict as a spectre of the collaborating church during Soviet times. Methodologically, this article analyses the role of individuals, key events, and documents in order to trace the processes that determined church-state relations in Russia from the end of the Soviet Union to the present.

MULTIPLE POST-SOVIET IDENTITIES: REPRESSION, COLLABORATION, DISSIDENCE, EMIGRATION

During the seventy years of the communist regime from 1917 to 1991, the life of the Russian Orthodox Church was marked by four distinct experiences: repression, collaboration, dissidence, and emigration (Stoeckl 2020a). *Repression* at the hands of the Bolshevik revolutionaries in the 1920s and 30s brought the Russian Orthodox Church to the brink of collapse through persecution of the faithful; executions of clergy members; the seizure of churches, monasteries and liturgical objects; and aggressive anti-religious propaganda. Even during the later decades of the Soviet regime, when religious persecution had become less bloody,

2 For a full bibliography, I refer readers to the original version of this article: Stoeckl, Kristina, "The Pact of the Old Guard: Religion, Law, and Politics for a Russia at War", Journal of Law and Religion, published online 2024: 1–12 (doi:10.1017/jlr.2024.22).

3 Russia's aggression against Ukraine started in 2014 with the annexation of the Crimea and Russia's support of separatist groups in eastern Ukraine. For reasons I discuss below, the attitude of the Church changed between 2014 and 2022.

the church continued to be unfree and remained under constant threat of new repressive measures. Faced with an omnipotent and omnipresent state, quite a few figures inside the Moscow Patriarchate chose the path of *collaboration* with the Soviet authorities and secret police, often in the belief that only in this way would the survival of the church itself be guaranteed. The current patriarch of Moscow, Kirill himself, collaborated with the KGB under the cover-name "Mikhailov" when he worked at the Department of External Church Relations during the 1970s (Saikali 2023). On the other side, among the faithful and clergy there were those who chose the path of *dissidence*, criticising the system and the church hierarchies that collaborated with the regime and bearing witness to Christian life in an environment hostile to all forms of religious expression.[4] Among them were, for example, the priest Gleb Yakunin, who denounced the collaboration of the church hierarchies (Kelly 1976), and the priest Alexander Men', whose Moscow parish included many intellectuals, among them the human rights activist Andrey Sakharov. The dissident voices could not count on support from the church hierarchies. Yakunin, in fact, was defrocked in the first half of the 1990s, and Alexander Men' was murdered under unclear circumstances in 1991.

Alongside these three models of religious life inside the Soviet Union there was a fourth experience that characterised the Russian Orthodox Church during communism, that of *emigration* to the West. Russian Orthodox immigrants to Western countries since 1917 frequently assumed the identity of guardians of the religious and cultural heritage banned from the homeland. Russian émigré theologians like Sergej Bulgakov and Georges Florovsky had a lasting impact on Orthodox theology. In the first half of the twentieth century, the theology of the Russian emigrants had to reckon with both the adverse conditions under which the mother church lived in the Soviet Union and the rise of fascism and Nazism in western Europe. In the post-war period, the heirs to the first generation of the Russian emigration, for example Alexander Schmemann, shaped the life and teaching of the Orthodox Church under conditions of religious pluralism in Western democratic and secular systems (Stoeckl 2007).

The collapse of the Soviet Union and the end of the Cold War allowed for a stocktaking of the various experiences that had marked Russian religious life in the past century: repression, collaboration, dissidence, emigration. In the face of these multiple experiences, different modes for defining its relationship with the state were available for the Russian Orthodox Church after 1991. It could define its post-Soviet identity in several ways: following the model of the Soviet-era dissidents and taking its cue from the experience of the emigrants living out their Orthodox faith in a democratic context, the church had the potential to be a witness to a flourishing faith under conditions of religious freedom, to advocate democratisation alongside civil society, and to raise a critical voice vis-à-vis the government. Alternatively, reconnecting with the imperial past and upholding the ties with the state created during the Soviet period, the church could opt for the model of a quasi-state church, take up the old Byzantine symphonic model, and define itself as a more cultural than religious rep-

4 The situation of Orthodox believers under communism was monitored by several institutions in the West, who documented religious freedom violations and maintained contact with dissidents, for example the Keston Institute in the UK, G2W in Switzerland and Russia Cristiana in Italy.

resentative of Russia's civil and political identity after communism.

For the first two decades of the post-communist transition, in fact, the Russian Orthodox Church followed all of these potential paths at one and the same time. Many scholars noticed the strong nationalist currents inside the church (Dunlop 1995) and pointed out fundamentalist and obscurantist tendencies (Shnirelman 2019; Mitrofanova 2005). However, these existed side by side with liberal trends (Knox 2004; Agadjanian 2013) and theological innovation and religious activism (Agadjanian 2003; Elsner 2023). For some time, the church leadership appeared to want to keep a balance between these different wings. In addition, the Moscow Patriarchate developed an active international agenda, which—albeit conservative—marked a departure from more traditional forms of anti-Westernism and anti-modernism inside the church (Stoeckl 2016). Post-Soviet Russian Orthodoxy was characterised by a multitude of identities and a high degree of ambivalence and multivocality, oscillating between freedom and control, nationalism and transnationalism, conveying different images of itself to believers, the Russian state, global Orthodoxy, and international politics. This multitude of roles was also reflected in church-state relations. Russia, as per its constitution, is a secular state. In the year 1990, at the height of perestroika, the government of the Russian Soviet Federative Socialist Republic passed a law on religious organisations which brought the country close to complete religious disestablishment and state religious neutrality. The law "prohibited the establishment of a state religion, and denied the state any right of intervention in religious affairs. Churches and other religious organizations were permitted to freely engage in worship and missionary activities, operate schools and seminaries, own property and publish religious literature, all without the requirement of registering with the government" (Davis 1997, 645). After the break-up of the Soviet Union, this law on religion retained validity and, during the first half of the 1990s, guaranteed the revival of religious life in Russia, including the emergence of new religious groups (Froese 2008). It was precisely the emergence of rival religious communities and the work of missionaries from abroad that aroused the disapproval of the Russian Orthodox Church, which demanded a change in legislation. The 1997 Law on Freedom of Conscience and Religious Associations reversed the trend of disestablishment and implemented a model of selective religion-state cooperation similar to many other European countries (Durham and Homer 1998; Davis 1997). In reality, however, the formal and informal practices of religious establishment in Russia were more complicated. Three distinct models of church-state relations coexisted: an unofficial state-church model, an official cooperation model, and an unofficial grassroots-led disestablishment model (Stoeckl 2020b). These three models are exemplified by the multiple strategies that church leaders and activists have pursued against abortion. First, the Patriarchate of Moscow symbolically interacted with the Kremlin as if the Russian Orthodox Church was a state church and representative of the country as such; second, ecclesiastical bureaucracy cooperated with state institutions on specific policy issues as if the Russian Orthodox believers were a minority in need of protection; and third, radical Orthodox activists saw themselves in a situation of disestablishment, in which the religious side was waging a "culture war" against the secular state. The case study of anti-abortion strategies shows that divergent trends of religious establishment existed inside the Russian Orthodox Church, and the church leadership composed of Patriarch Kirill and his circle represented only one (albeit powerful) factor.

In terms of religious identity and religion-state relations, therefore, the first two decades after the end of communism in Russia were a period of different potential pathways and multiple roles for the church. The situation started to change in the third decade of post-communism: the year 2009 saw the inauguration of Kirill as patriarch of Moscow; in May 2008, Nikolaj Patrushev switched from his role as head of the FSB (the former KGB) to directing the Security Council of Russia; and in 2012, Putin took up office as president of the Russian Federation for a third time. Under their influence, the Russian state and the Russian Orthodox Church moved closer to each other in ways that had less to do with religion and more with legislation, politics and power.

CONSOLIDATING CHURCH-STATE RELATIONS THROUGH LAW

The 1997 Law on Freedom of Conscience and Religious Associations, which regulates the relationship between the Russian Orthodox Church and the Russian state, has remained substantially unchanged, but a series of other legislative provisions between 2010 and 2021 have defined the role and place of the Russian Orthodox Church vis-à-vis the Russian state in increasingly narrow terms. The 1997 law distinguished between "traditional religions" and "non-traditional religions and sects" (Daniel and Marsh 2007; Shterin and Richardson 1998) and granted a protected legal status only to the former: Orthodox Christianity, Islam, Judaism, and Buddhism. Recognising in its preamble "the special contribution of Orthodoxy to the history of Russia and to the establishment and development of Russia's spirituality and culture" (Daniel and Marsh 2007, 8), the law explicitly identified Orthodoxy with the Russian national identity and memory. This definition, and especially the term tradition, subsequently became a recurrent theme in legislative texts, starting with Russia's National Security Concept. The initial version in 2000, prepared by the first presidential administration of Vladimir Putin, introduced a connection between "traditions" and state security: "Assurance of the Russian Federation's national security also includes protecting the cultural and spiritual-moral legacy and the historical traditions and standards of public life, and preserving the cultural heritage of all Russia's people" (Payne 2010, 713). In all the subsequent iterations of the National Security Concept of the Russian Federation—2009, 2015, and 2021—which were worked out under the leadership of Patrushev, "traditional Russian spiritual and moral values" are cited as an integral part of Russia's national security strategy (Stoeckl 2022a; Official English website of the Kremlin 2021).[5]

Besides *tradition and spiritual and moral values*, a new concept—*religious feelings*—was introduced in 2012 in the aftermath of the Pussy-Riot case, when a group of female performers enacted a "punk prayer" inside Moscow's Cathedral of Christ the Saviour (Uzlaner 2014). At the time the Pussy Riot group came to trial, the Russian penal code did not yet include a suitable paragraph for "blasphemy", and the band-members were convicted on "hooliganism" charges. The Russian

5 The latest edition of the Russian National Security Strategy can be found here: http://www.kremlin.ru/acts/bank/47046

Duma subsequently amended Article 148 of the Russian Federation Criminal Code "in the aim of protecting religious convictions and feelings of citizens against insults". The amendment included a maximum penalty for such offences: imprisonment for up to one year, and, if the offence was committed in a place of worship, up to three years (Official English website of the Kremlin 2013). From the sociological perspective, one could say that after semantically framing the Orthodox Church's teachings in macro-sociological terms as *tradition and spiritual and moral values*, this new legislative step added a micro-sociological dimension: *feelings*. The law against "insulting religious feelings" strengthened the power-conforming, patriotic, and conservative camp inside the Church and sidelined liberal or simply apolitical believers (Uzlaner and Stoeckl 2019, 434). The law also had a disruptive potential that became apparent when, only a few years later, Orthodox extremists used the argument of religious insult to attack the film *Matilda* about the life of Tsar Nicholas II. The activists took issue with the portrayal of a love affair between the tsar (who has been canonised by the Russian Orthodox Church) and a ballet dancer. The offended believers, who in the previous case had huddled under the protective wing of the Russian state prosecutor, started to act on their own—to the point of an open confrontation with state and church authorities. In the *Matilda* case, the offended believers stopped being the silent majority under the supervision and protection of the church and state. They became a shouting minority which turned into a headache for both secular and church authorities, who started to distance themselves from the overly offended believers, insisting that they were not true believers, but "pseudo-religious radicals" (Tass 2017). However, whether overly or insufficiently offended, the law against "hurting religious feelings" gave the church leadership and the state an instrument to define who is a legitimate Orthodox believer and who is not.

The final legislative process that is relevant in this short overview of defining Orthodox identity by means of law and politics is the constitutional amendment of 2020. The main purpose of the amendment to the Russian Constitution of 2020 was to guarantee Putin the possibility of two more terms in office, but the constitutional process was also notable with regard to the role of the church. In the lead-up to the constitutional reform, Patriarch Kirill promoted the idea of including the word "God" in the preamble of the constitution, following the example of the national anthem of the Russian Federation (Interfax 2020b). The national anthem uses the melody of the old Soviet anthem, with a text from 2000 that includes the verse "Russia – Our holy nation [...] God-protected homeland!", which actually echoes a passus in the Orthodox liturgy: "We pray to the Lord for our God-protected country." The committee responsible for constitutional amendments was not ready to accept the suggestion, and the preamble remained unchanged. Instead, a new paragraph 67-1(2) was inserted, which reads: "The Russian Federation, united by a thousand-year history, preserving the memory of the ancestors who passed on to us the ideals and faith in God, as well as the continuity in the development of the Russian state, recognizes the historically established state unity" (Konstitutsiya Rossijskoj Federatsii 2020). Religion—faith in God—was defined by the legislator as a quality of "ancestors" and a part of national history. Another constitutional amendment promoted by church circles was the definition of marriage as being only between a man and a woman in order to create a barrier to the legalisation of same-sex marriages (Interfax 2020a). The proposal came from Konstantin Malofeev, the conservative oligarch and, as of 2018, deputy chairman of the ultranationalist organisation the World Russian People's Council. He was immediately echoed by the spokesman for the Moscow Patriarchate Vladimir Legoida, who added a fourth item to the church's list of constitutional desiderata, namely "traditional family values" (Ria Novosti 2020). Both additions were included in the amended constitution. Paragraph 72(1) now includes "defense of the institution of marriage as the union of one man and one woman", and paragraph 114(1) lists the "preservation of traditional family values" among the goals of the Russian Federation (Konstitutsiya Rossijskoj Federatsii).

To summarise this overview of the legislative steps that have defined the identity and role of the Russian Orthodox Church in Russian society between roughly 2010 and 2021: despite the fact that the constitutional arrangement of Russia as a secular state with a regime of selective religion-state cooperation has remained formally unchanged since 1997, legislative and political processes have gradually tightened the normative framework around the Russian Orthodox Church and believers. The church has been defined as a bearer of Russian statehood and national security, and believers have been framed as either potential victims of insult or potential extremists. Inside a church thus defined, there is no space for protest against the state but ample room for patronising and bullying believers and clerics. For the patriarch of Moscow, the narrowing down of options for believers and for the church's role inside society was probably a welcome result, because it promised control over the messy and pluralist church of the post-Soviet decades. The political leaders in charge, President Putin and the secretary of Russia's Security Council and former FSB director Patrushev (who was removed from his position in the Security Council in May 2024 and now holds another influential position as an assistant of President Putin), could now rely on the church as a provider of a traditionalist agenda and edifying symbolism around Russian statehood. These three men are representative of a leadership steeped in a Soviet logic of authority, control, obedience, and friend-enemy thinking. The old guard worked towards winding back the freedoms, imbalances, and contradictions that the end of the Soviet Union had created both within Russian society and inside the church. They did so through repressive measures, control of information, and the creation of a new, all-encompassing ideology built around traditional values.

THE INTEGRATION OF CHURCH AND STATE THROUGH WAR

With hindsight, the autocephaly of the Orthodox Church of Ukraine in 2018 was the tipping point with regard to the Orthodox Church's relative openness to different scenarios and roles within Russian society. Prior to 2018, several church formations present inside Ukraine had tried, in vain, to be recognised as "canonical" by the other Orthodox churches. In the absence of global Orthodoxy's support for these groups, the Moscow Patriarchate continued to claim exclusive canonical jurisdiction over Ukraine (Denysenko 2018). From 2014 onwards, the annexation of Crimea and the war in Donbas fuelled radical forces inside the Russian Orthodox Church (Hovorun 2014). The granting of autocephaly to the

Orthodox Church of Ukraine by the Ecumenical Patriarchate in 2018 became the tipping point. The Moscow Patriarchate entered into an open conflict with the Ecumenical Patriarchate and emerged, on the whole, weakened, despite the fact that most parishes in Ukraine initially remained with the Ukrainian Orthodox Church of the Moscow Patriarchate. The autocephaly of the Orthodox Church of Ukraine radicalised the ecclesiastical leadership. With the onset of Russia's full-scale war against Ukraine in February 2022 and the display of unconditional loyalty of the patriarch of Moscow to the goals of the war ("the special military operation" in official language), the relative openness of the Orthodox Church to different scenarios and roles within Russian society ended. The arrests of believers and defrocking of priests who protested against the war, with which I started my introduction, are clear indicators that the multivocal Russian Orthodox Church, which had been in the making since the end of the Soviet Union, has been put back into the bottle of tight ideological control.

Patriarch Kirill invested all of his authority in legitimising the war in Ukraine: on 6 March 2022, Forgiveness Sunday in the Orthodox tradition, the patriarch of Moscow preached that the world is divided between two forces, one good and divine, the other evil and sinful. Powerful forces, he said, were coercing Russia and its Orthodox believers to stray from the path of righteousness by imposing on them a regime of liberties, the final and most terrible of which was the holding of gay parades. In the patriarch's eyes, Ukraine was the Orthodox world that was being threatened by the evil West, and Russia was coming to its rescue (Official website of the Moscow Patriarchate 2022a). Already on 27 February 2022, the patriarch had expressed the view that Russia, Belarus and Ukraine were one entity: he used the medieval term Rus' to refer to the three countries. By defining Ukraine as "Russia", the patriarch was not only following the viewpoint of the Russian president, who had denied Ukraine's sovereign existence; he also defined Russia's attack on Ukraine as an act of self-defence of the Rus' against evil Western forces, allegedly at work in Ukraine. On 7 April 2022, the patriarch celebrated the liturgy in the cathedral of the Russian Armed Forces in Moscow's Patriot Park. He said it was the role of the Orthodox to withstand the coming of the Antichrist and called on the nation "to wake up and recognize that a time has come that can determine the historic destiny of our nation" (Official website of the Moscow Patriarchate 2022b). In September 2022, he wholeheartedly supported the partial mobilisation of Russian men to the armed forces and compared their fight to the struggle of the medieval Rus' against the Mongol Golden Horde of 1380 (Official website of the Moscow Patriarchate 2022d). He even promised soldiers forgiveness for all their sins for their sacrifice in battle. But the patriarch did not only pray for the Russian armed forces, he also exhorted believers to include President Putin in their prayers (Official website of the Moscow Patriarchate 2022c). Also in its external relations, especially with the Vatican, the Russian Orthodox Church clearly supported the Russian state—to the point that Pope Francis called Kirill "an altar boy" of Putin (Reuters 2022). The patriarch has consistently shown support for the war through expressing and nurturing a worldview in which the war is not only legitimate but necessary, and ultimately in accordance with God's will (Horsfjord 2024).

The warmongering of the patriarch culminated in a declaration by the

World Russian People's Council in March 2024, in which the war in Ukraine is called "a holy war". The World Russian People's Council organisation is closely tied to the Moscow Patriarchate without being an ecclesiastical institution. With the patriarch of Moscow as statutory president and directed by Konstantin Malofeev since 2018, the council has a history of promoting ultrapatriotic positions. The declaration of March 2024 was in line with positions previously expressed by Malofeev, but it represented a new level of inflammatory language from the side of Patriarch Kirill. The document included the sentence "The special military operation is a Holy War, in which Russia and its people, defending the single spiritual space of Holy Rus', fulfill the mission of "the Restrainer" [Missiyu Удерживающего], protecting the world from the onslaught of globalism and the victory of the West, which has fallen into Satanism" (Official website of the Moscow Patriarchate 2024). The term "restrainer" is a reference to the *katehon*, from the Greek word 'the one who withholds'. The idea that the Russian nation is a modern day *katehon* against Western liberalism and secularism has been a common theme for Russian nationalist ideology for over a decade (Hagemeister 2016; Suslov 2014; Shnirelman 2024). This nationalist ideology has now become the official position of the Moscow Patriarchate.

Meanwhile, the Russian state has been delivering one document after another that ties Russian state ideology to the traditional values promoted by the Russian Orthodox Church. On 9 November 2022, Putin signed a decree entitled "Fundamentals of the State Policy for the Preservation and Strengthening of Traditional Russian Spiritual and Moral Values". Among the aims laid out in the document was the cooperation of state bodies with the media and various channels of communication with the aim of popularising and promoting traditional values and the creation of an image of the Russian state on the international stage as a "keeper and protector of traditional universal human spiritual and moral values" (Official website of the Kremlin 2022). This decree was followed by a revised Russian foreign policy strategy, which included the strategic collaboration between the state, the Russian Orthodox Church and other traditional religions (Official website of the Kremlin 2023). In his speeches, Putin repeated the talking points regularly used by the patriarch in his sermons: the West's departure from traditional values, the destruction of family, cultural and national identity in the West, perversion and abuse of children, paedophilia, and same-sex marriages. According to Putin, "millions of people in the West" also thought that they were being led into a "spiritual disaster" and were looking to Russia with hope (Official English website of the Kremlin 2023).

After the inauguration ceremony for his fifth term as president of the Russian Federation on 7 May 2024, Putin and Patriarch Kirill convened at the Kremlin's Annunciation Cathedral for a solemn prayer, during which Kirill compared Putin to Saint Alexander Nevsky. The symbolism of their encounter was that of a modern-day symphony of state and church: Putin, like the tsars of the Russian Empire in the past, blessed by the patriarch.

A STATE WITHOUT FREE ELECTIONS AND A CHURCH WITHOUT FREEDOM OF PRAYER

The image of President Putin and Patriarch Kirill in the Kremlin's Annunciation Cathedral was emblematic for the pact of the old guard:

the two men standing united at the top of a state without free elections and a church without freedom of prayer. Putin, Kirill and the circle around them represent a worldview guided by post-Soviet revanchism, Russian nationalism, and militarism. In this worldview, the church is the provider of ritual and spiritual wrappings for autocratic, imperial politics. The course of events analysed in this article has determined a dramatic closure of the potential pathways of Russian Orthodoxy. The first two decades after the collapse of the Soviet Union had been characterised by a multiplicity of forms of religious life inside the Russian Orthodox Church. The Soviet period had marked the life of the Russian Orthodox Church in four different ways—repression, collaboration, dissidence, and emigration. Over the last decades, these experiences have inspired different ways of living out the Orthodox faith in the post-Soviet context. For example, the Memorial organisation, winner of the 2022 Nobel Peace Prize, was founded to keep the memory of repression alive. It was declared a foreign agent in 2015 and closed in 2021 at the behest of the Kremlin, which seeks to silence this part of Russia's collective memory. Orthodox priests and faithful worshippers continue to find inspiration in the example of dissidence, like the priest Ioann Koval who was punished for changing the word "victory" to "peace" in a prayer. Finally, many Orthodox priests and believers who have left Russia after 2022 now make up the new emigration (e.g. Kordochkin 2023). Of all potential roles for his church, Patriarch Kirill has pursued the one he knew best: collaboration. On the side of the state, Putin and his like also continued what they knew best: provide a state ideology, identify an enemy, and sanctify the state. The pact of the old guard is backward-looking, but it determines, for now, the future of Russians, Ukrainians and the rest of the world.

BIBLIOGRAPHY

Agadjanian, A. (2003) The Social Vision of Russian Orthodoxy: Balancing between Identity and Relevance, *Orthodox Christianity and Contemporary Europe*, edited by J. Sutton and W. van den Bercken. Leuven, Paris, Dudley: Peeters, 163–182.

Agadjanian, A. (2013) Reform and Revival in Moscow Orthodox Communities. Two Types of Religious Modernity, *Archives de Sciences Sociales des Religions* 162, 75–94.

Chapnin, S. (2023) An Act of Lighthearted Betrayal, *Public Orthodoxy*. 12 May 2023. https://publicorthodoxy.org/2023/05/12/act-of-lighthearted-betrayal/ (Last accessed 12 February 2025).

Daniel, W. L. and Marsh, C. (2007) Russia's 1997 Law on Freedom of Conscience in Context and Retrospect, *Journal of Church and State* 49 (1), 5–17.

Davis, D. H. (1997) Russia's New Law on Religion: Progress or Regress?, *Journal of Church and State* 39, 645–46.

Denysenko, N. E. (2018) *The Orthodox Church in Ukraine: A Century of Separation*. DeKalb, IL: Northern Illinois University Press.

Dunlop, J. B. (1995) The Russian Orthodox Church as an "Empire-Saving" Institution, *The Politics of Religion in Russia and the New States of Eurasia*, edited by M. Bourdeaux Armonk. New York: M. E. Sharpe, 15–41.

Durham, W. C. and Homer, L. B. (1998), Russia's 1997 Law on Freedom of Conscience and Religious Associations: An Analytical Appraisal, *Emory International Law Review* 12 (101), 101–246.

Elsner, R. (2023) Questioning the Concept of "Religious Activism" in Russian Orthodoxy from a Theological Perspective, *Religion, State and Society* 51 (1),30–48.

Froese, P. (2008) *The Plot to Kill God: Findings from the Soviet Experiment in Secularization*. Berkeley and Los Angeles: University of California Press.

Hagemeister, M. (2016) Der Nördliche Katechon – Neobyzantismus und Politischer Hesychasmus im Postsowjetischen Russland, *Erfurter Vorträge zur Kulturgeschichte des Orthodoxen Christentums* 15, 38 pages.

Horsfjord, V. L. (2024) Patriarch and Patriot: History in Patriarch Kirill's Sermons in the First Year of the Full-Scale War in Ukraine, *Religion, State and Society*, 52 (4), 367–382.

Hovorun, C. (2014) The Church in the Bloodlands, *First Things*. 1 October 2014, 41–44.

Interfax (2020a) V Konstitutsiiu predlozhili vnesti polozhenie o sem'e kak soiuze muzhchiny i zhenshchiny [Proposal to introduce a provision on the family as a union of a man and a woman into the Constitution]. *Interfax*. 30 January 2020. https://www.interfax.ru/russia/693381 (Last accessed 12 February 2025).

Interfax (2020b) Patriarkh Kirill predlozhil vklyuchit' upominanie o boge v Konstitutsiyu Rossii [Patriarch Kirill suggests to include a reference to God in the Russian Constitution]. *Interfax*. 1 February 2020. https://www.interfax.ru/russia/693665 (Last accessed 12 February 2025).

Interfax (2023) Patriarkh Kirill zapretil v sluzhenii svyashchenika, zanimavshegosya voprosom 'Troitsy' Rubleva [Patriarch Kirill banned the priest who dealt with the issue of Rublev's Trinity from serving]. *Interfax*. 27 May 2023. https://www.interfax.ru/russia/903521 (Last accessed 12 February 2025).

Kelly, D. (1976) Nairobi: A Door Opened, *Religion in Communist Lands* 4 (1), 4–17.

Knox, Z. (2004) *Russian Society and the Orthodox Church: Religion in Russia after Communism.* New York, London: Routledge.

Konstitutsiya Rossijskoj Federatsii [Constitution of the Russian Federation]. *Rossijskaja gazeta No. 144 (8198)*. 4 June 2020. https://rg.ru/2020/07/04/konstituciya-site-dok.html (Last accessed 12 February 2025).

Kordochkin, A. (2023) Letter to Russia: The Importance of Finding Those Who Are United in Spirit, *Public Orthodoxy*. 30 November 2023. https://publicorthodoxy.org/2023/11/30/letter-to-russia/ (Last accessed 12 February 2025).

Mitrofanova, A. V. (2005), *The Politicization of Russian Orthodoxy: Actors and Ideas.* Stuttgart: Ibidem.

Official English website of the Kremlin (2013) Amendment to Criminal Code and certain legislative acts in the aim of protecting religious convictions and feelings. *Official website of the Kremlin*. 30 June 2013. http://www.en.kremlin.ru/acts/news/18422 (Last accessed 12 February 2025).

Official English website of the Kremlin (2023) Presidential Address to Federal Assembly. *Official website of the Kremlin*. 21 February 2023. http://en.kremlin.ru/events/president/transcripts/70565 (Last accessed 12 February 2025).

Official website of the Kremlin (2021) Ukaz Prezidenta Rossiiskoi Federatsii ot 02.07.2021 N° 400 'O Strategii Natsional'noi Bezopasnosti Rossiiskoi Federatsii' [Decree of the President of the Russian Federation on July 2, 2021 No. 400 On the National Security Strategy of the Russian Federation]. *Official website of the Kremlin*. 2 July 2021. http://www.kremlin.ru/acts/bank/47046 (Last accessed 12 February 2025).

Official website of the Kremlin (2022) Osnov gosudarstvennoy politiki po sokhraneniyu i ukrepleniyu traditsionnykh rossiyskikh dukhovno-nravstvennykh tsennostey [Fundamentals of the State Policy for the Preservation and Strengthening of Traditional Russian Spiritual and Moral Values]. *Official website of the Kremlin*. 9 November 2022. http://kremlin.ru/acts/news/69810 (Last accessed 12 February 2025).

Official website of the Kremlin (2023) Ukaz ob utverzhdenii Kontseptsii vneshney politiki Rossiyskoy Federatsii [Decree on approval of the Foreign Policy Concept of the Russian Federation]. *Official website of the Kremlin*. 31 March 2023. http://kremlin.ru/events/president/news/70811 (Last accessed 12 February 2025).

Official website of the Moscow Patriarchate (2022a) Patriarshaya propoved' v Nedelyu syropustnuyu posle Liturgii v Khrame Khrista Spasitelya [Patriarchal sermon on Forgiveness Sunday in the Christ Saviour Cathedral]. *Official Website of the Moscow Patriarchate*. 6 March 2022. http://www.patriarchia.ru/db/text/5962628.html (Last accessed 12 February 2025).

Official website of the Moscow Patriarchate (2022b) Slovo Svyateyshego Patriarkha Kirilla v Nedelyu 4-yu Velikogo posta posle Liturgii v glavnom khrame Vooruzhennykh sil RF [Patriarchal sermon on the third Sunday of Great Lent after the liturgy in the main church of the armed forces of the Russian Federation]. *Official Website of the Moscow Patriarchate*. 3 April 2022. http://www.patriarchia.ru/db/text/5914188.html (Last accessed 12 February 2025).

Official website of the Moscow Patriarchate (2022c) Slovo Svyateyshego Patriarkha Kirilla v den' pamyati blagovernykh knyazey Daniila Moskovskogo i Aleksandra Nevskogo posle Liturgii v Danilovom monastyre [Patriarchal Sermon on the day of remembrance of the blessed princes Daniil of Moscow and Alexander Nevsky after the liturgy in the Danilov Monastery]. *Official website of the Moscow Patriarchate*. 12 September 2022. http://www.patriarchia.ru/db/text/5958411.html (Last accessed 12 February 2025).

Official website of the Moscow Patriarchate (2022d) Slovo Svyateyshego Patriarkha Kirilla v prazdnik Rozhdestva Presvyatoy Bogoroditsy posle Liturgii v Zachat'yevskom stavropigial'nom monastyre g. Moskvy [Patriarchal sermon on the Feast of the Nativity of the Blessed Virgin Mary after the liturgy in the Conception Stavropegic Monastery in Moscow]. *Official website of the Moscow Patriarchate*. 21 September 2022. http://www.patriarchia.ru/db/text/5961645.html (Last accessed 12 February 2025).

Official website of the Moscow Patriarchate (2024) Наказ XXV Всемирного русского народного собора «Настоящее и будущее Русского мира». *Official website of the Moscow Patriarchate*. 27 March 2024. http://www.patriarchia.ru/db/text/6116189.html (Last accessed 12 February 2025).

Payne, D. P. (2010) Spiritual Security, the Russian Orthodox Church, and the Russian Foreign Ministry: Collaboration or Cooptation?, *Journal of Church and State* 52 (4), 712–727.

Ria Novosti (2020) V RPTs podderzhali ideiu o popravke v Konstitutsiiu po zashchite sem'I [The Russian Orthodox Church supported the idea of an amendment to the Constitution to protect the family]. *Ria Novosti*. 14 February 2020. https://ria.ru/20200214/1564802300.html (Last accessed 12 February 2025).

Reuters (2022) Pope Wants to Visit Moscow to Meet Putin Over Ukraine. *Reuters*. 4 May 2022. https://www.reuters.com/world/europe/pope-says-wants-go-moscow-meet-putin-over-ukraine-paper-2022-05-03/ (Last accessed 12 February 2025).

Saikali, E. (2023) Patriarch Kirill: The Politically Influential Head of the Russian Orthodox Church, *France 24*. 9 January 2023. https://www.france24.com/en/europe/20230109-patriarch-kirill-the-politically-influential-head-of-the-russian-orthodox-church (Last accessed 12 February 2025).

Shnirelman, V. (2019) Russian Neoconservatism and Apocalyptic Imperialism, *Contemporary Russian Conservatism: Problems, Paradoxes and Dangers*, edited by M. Suslov and D. Uzlaner. Leiden: Brill, 347–378.

Shnirelman, V. (2024) Russia as Katechon: Civilizationalism and Eschatological Discourse in Putin's Russia, *RussiaPost*. 1 July 2024. https://russiapost.info/society/katechon (Last accessed 12 February 2025).

Shterin, M. S. and Richardson, J. T. (1998) Local Laws Restricting Religion in Russia: Precursors of Russia's New National Law, *Journal of Church and State* 40 (2), 319–341.

Stoeckl, K. (2007) The Lesson of the Revolution in Russian Émigré Theology and Contemporary Orthodox Thought, *Religion, State and Society* 35 (4), 285–300.

Stoeckl, K. (2016) The Russian Orthodox Church as Moral Norm Entrepreneur, *Religion, State & Society* 44 (2), 131–151.

Stoeckl, K. (2020a) *Russian Orthodoxy and Secularism*. Leiden: Brill.

Stoeckl, K. (2020b) Three Models of Church-State Relations in Contemporary Russia, *Constitutions and Religion*, edited by S. Mancini. Camberley Surrey: Edward Elgar, 237–252.

Stoeckl, K. (2022) Russia's Spiritual Security Doctrine as a Challenge to European Comprehensive Security Approaches, *The Review of Faith & International Affairs* 20 (4), 37–44.

Stoeckl, K. (2024) The Pact of the Old Guard: Religion, Law, and Politics for a Russia at War, *Journal of Law and Religion*, 1–12. DOI: https://doi.org/10.1017/jlr.2024.22)

Suslov, M. (2014) Holy Rus': The Geopolitical Imagination in the Contemporary Russian Orthodox Church, *Russian Politics & Law* 53 (3), 67–88.

Tass (2017) Legoida: sviazannye s fil'mom 'Matil'da' akty nasiliia ne mogut iskhodit'ot veruiushchikh [Legoida: acts of violence around Matilda cannot be connected to believers]. Tass: Information Agency. 11 September 2017. https://tass.ru/obschestvo/4553987 (Last accessed 12 February 2025).

Uzlaner, D. (2014) The Pussy Riot Case and the Peculiarities of Russian Post-Secularism, *State, Religion and Church* 1 (1), 23–58.

Uzlaner, D. and Stoeckl, K. (2019) From Pussy Riot's "Punk Prayer" to Matilda: Orthodox Believers, Critique, and Religious Freedom in Russia, *Journal of Contemporary Religion* 34 (3), 427–445.